AMAZING GRACE

An Understanding of God's Great Love for Us

Power Living Ministries
Anaheim, California

Amazing Grace
An Understanding of God's Great Love for Us
ISBN 0-9626910-2-X
Copyright © 1993 by
Tom Barkey
1026 S. East Street
Anaheim, CA 92805
U.S.A.

Published by
Power Living Ministries
1026 S. East Street
Anaheim, CA 92805

DEDICATION

Power Living Ministries is committed to helping people understand God's love and grace. A very special group of people have this vision and have made this book available to you at no cost. This book is dedicated to them:

Joanna Aguilar
Rosalinda Aguilar
Gill and Char Alfaro
Kent and Mary Ann Almgren
Daniel and Tracy Amstutz
Guy and Lois Bailey
Tom and Linda Barkey
Jim and Mary Barndollar
Bob Bell
Mark and Nancy Boucher
Dan and Rita Brown
Joe and Lucille Burns
Virginia Clark
Janice DeMola
Helen DeSutter
Jay and Barb Felgar
Pat and Sandy Finney
Jim and Minerva Glass
Tracy Gould
Roger and Meridith Greear
Ron Greiner
Gil and Jeanne Guzman
Kevin and Carrie Haag
Larry and Corina Harper
John and Katherine Hesford
Cheryl Hesford
Howard A. Heins Trust
Bud and Virginia Hughes
Ken and Mer Jacobs
Sherry Jones

Allen and Jan Kriz
Nancy LaCasse
Elwyn and Mavis Lewis
Cliff and Louise Lotzenhiser
Clifford and Carolyn Lotzenhiser
David and Dianna Lotzenhiser
Fran Lundquist
Debbie Martel
Deborah Mayhew
John and Eltha McConnell
Van and June McKinzie
Chris and Gay Meador
Rod and Philomine Moore
David and Ann Nicholes
Joe and Olga Otanez
Richard and Valeeta Pharr
Bob and Joanne Pipes
Jim and Kathy Robbins
Craig and Diane Ross
Jay and Dee Santos
Edward and Mary Simone
Tom and LaVonne Smith
Dave and Toni Stannard
Lee and Mary Thompson
Myriam Toro
Michael and Pamela Tucker
LeRoy and Beverly Watson
Andy and Valerie Williams
Tom and Wendi Wineland

ACKNOWLEDGMENT

Through the help of the Holy Spirit, this book was prepared by many skilled individuals. I would like to give special acknowledgment for their help and support in making it possible. They are the following people: Beth Parker, for the many hours of transcribing, editing, and encouragement; Joan Peart, Mark Boucher, and Gay Meador, for their tireless reading and rereading of the manuscripts; Dawn Klein, for her help on the drawings and typesetting; and Genadi Ponomarenko, for his wonderful, creative gift on the cover design.

CONTENTS

Acknowledgment

Dedication

Introduction . . . . *vii*

1   How Much Does He Really Love Us? 1

2   The Love of God in Action 9

3   Can God Love Me? 19

4   Righteousness: A Two-Way Relationship 27

5   He Took It All Away 35

6   Submission v. Chastisement 41

7   Relationship by Faith, Not Works 49

8   The Judgment of Sin 55

9   Performance Lifestyle 59

10   The Spiritual Believer 63

About the Power Living Ministries 71

About the Author 72

INTRODUCTION

You are about to embark upon a spiritual journey. If you will allow every word of this teaching to sink into your mind, you will be changed for the rest of your life.

I believe this is the most important message from the Bible. As a pastor, in all of the adults I have ministered to over the years, I've found their biggest problem hasn't been their problem. It has been their lack of understanding and belief that God loves them personally, and has not rejected them.

Several years ago, I found myself in a place of despair. I was going to quit the ministry. I felt like I was a hypocrite. The reason I felt like a hypocrite was because I was preaching a legalistic gospel that I could not live up to myself.

I found myself saying, "God, I don't understand how to relate with You, how to live in this relationship with You." I found myself always trying to please God but never really accomplishing it. I was always trying to do more for God's Kingdom but never felt like I did enough, always praying a lot but never praying enough, always giving but never giving enough.

I was falling apart; I was breaking down. I went to the Lord in prayer and asked Him for something that would change my life. Otherwise, I would have to quit the ministry. The Spirit of the Lord began to lead me into a five-year study of His grace. It has brought me to the place that I now understand, "This is who I am and God loves me." He looks at my past, and He loves me; He looks at my future, and He loves me. If I yield to Him, *His will* will be done in my life.

Have you gone through some difficult things in your past? Maybe you've experienced an abortion, a rape, a divorce, a death of someone close to you, or a rejection of some kind. Maybe you just feel "messed up" in life. Do you come from a dysfunctional family, perhaps with incest, physical abuse, or mental abuse?

Without this message, you won't fully recover. With this message, you will be on the road to deliverance, recovery, and healing.

Years ago, Martin Luther was so moved by God that he said, "I'm going to go against the tide of tradition and declare that 'the just shall live by faith.' " Martin Luther began what is now known as The Reformation.

Just as with Martin Luther, I feel a call of God on me to go *against the tide of legalism in the Church today* and declare, "We too, shall live by faith, but **in the grace of God and not by works**." I have a conviction from the Holy Spirit that people absolutely must understand that God loves them *personally.* You'll be without peace for years until you finally grasp the ultimate love that God has for you, and how He wants you to succeed in life.

If God said to me, "Tom, you can only preach one message for the rest of your life, so pick it, then I will send you out on the road to preach it to people everywhere," this is what I'd choose: a message that would show how much God cares for you and loves you. I would introduce you to **Father God.**

Tom Barkey

CHAPTER 1

How Much Does He Really Love Us?

How much does God love people? We all know that "God loves the world." Unfortunately, a lot of people don't count themselves as a part of "the world." They say "God loves the world, but if everyone knew what I was really like, they would know that God doesn't really care too much for me."

I want you to know how much God loves you personally. And, I want you to understand that God is working in your life out of grace, and not out of works.

To fully understand God's love for you, we must go back to the beginning.

Genesis 1:26-27   Then God said, "Let Us make man in Our image, according to Our likeness; let them have dominion over the fish of the sea, over the birds of the air, and over the cattle, over all the earth and over every creeping thing that creeps on the earth." So God created man in His own image; in the image of God He created him; male and female He created them.

GOD←→MAN

God and man had a face to face relationship

God and man now have a relationship. They have companionship; they have fellowship. They're able to talk one on one. Man was able to see God face to face then. He was walking and talking with God. He was in the very presence of God.

There is a relationship between God and man at this point: a love relationship. God actually created the earth and said, "Man, I give you dominion over this whole earth."

God gave man everything in the earth except one thing. He said there was only one thing that He didn't want man to do: eat of the tree of the knowledge of good and evil.

Genesis 2:17   "but of the tree of the knowledge of good and evil, you shall not eat, for in the day that you eat of it, you shall surely die."

God loved man so much, He said, "I have created the universe, earth, land, water, animals, birds, fish, and vegetation—you can have it all." Through God's giving of the complete ownership of everything, we can see how much He loves man. Now that is some kind of love.

But, we know the story: Adam and Eve ate of the fruit of the tree. A serpent came up to them in the garden. The serpent deceived Eve. The Bible says the woman was deceived, but the man was not. The woman ate of the tree, she fell; man took the fruit from her and he ate it, he fell. Now we have the "fall of man."

In your mental picture of the fall of man, you need to understand a few things. The sin that Adam committed was idolatry: the worship of himself. He literally committed treason by rebelling against God.

Man is no longer in God's fellowship. A very large gap between God and man exists.

GOD

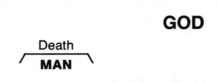

Man is dead to God

Now sin controls man's life instead of faith. A very negative controlling factor has come into his life: sin. Sin now dictates his life and man becomes a prisoner to his fate.

GOD

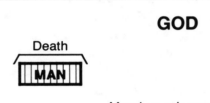

Man is a prisoner to sin

But in the midst of this fall, God gave a prophetic word in Genesis 3. The seed of the woman will come and crush the head of the serpent. God gave this prophetic word about Jesus Who would come and die on the cross to redeem man.

GOD

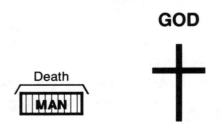

But until that time, man was a prisoner. We must understand that the woman, the man, the serpent, and the earth were all cursed. The once-perfect earth now starts to change and the curse begins: reverse evolution. The earth starts to decay and has continued to do so until today. It is literally falling apart.

The environmentalists today who want to save the earth, cannot, because it's falling apart. Jesus came to save man, not the earth. But God has it all under control. He has a plan. We don't have to worry about some man somewhere pushing a button to blow up the earth, because God Himself is going to blow it up someday. After God completes His plan, the Bible says in II Peter 3:10 that God destroys the earth. Then He creates a new earth and a new heaven. But until that time, believers are waiting and serving God.

How Do We Know That God Loves Us?

After man sinned, why didn't God just make "crispy critters" of them? Why didn't He just start over with new dust?

God looked at man in his fallen state, and said, "I'm in love with you, and I want to redeem you. I want to help you." In the New Testament, man is declared to be God's enemy. He's now serving sin; He's serving another god (sin) while in his prison. This other god is now controlling him, demanding that he behave in a certain anti-God fashion.

Before the fall, God said, "I want a relationship of love. I will respect and love you, and you will respect and love Me. We will have fellowship together."

After the fall, the god of this world says, "I don't care about you. I insist that you behave my way. I demand certain things to be done in your flesh."

God certainly had the right to judge Adam and Eve, didn't He? He could have eliminated them. Don't you think God had the right to get mad at them and say, "Look what you did!'' But God still looked at them with eyes of love, and He decided to do something about it.

Was God Fair?

I remember when I was young, our family hated our neighbors. I mean we hated them so much that we had dug a long ditch on the property line to separate their yard from our yard. "This is our grass, that is your grass, so stay over there." The kids in our family fought with the kids in their family, and our parents fought too. After a period of time, the feud stopped and we all forgot what we were fighting about.

Have you ever hated anybody? Don't you think that if somebody used or abused you, hatred for them would come into your life? It's a natural reaction, isn't it? Well, here's Adam who had everything he could ever need from God, but he abused God and took what was not his.

The Bible says that Adam was not deceived (I Timothy 2:14). I would like to tell you my belief about what happened at the fall of man.

I believe the woman was deceived. She really felt that if she ate of the fruit of the tree, she would have been like God. I believe that her motive was "I can be just like God and help Him." I believe that her motive was pure. She thought she was doing something right and good.

Her motive made her innocent, so the fall wasn't the woman's fault. But the Bible says Adam wasn't deceived; he knew he was going to fall from the presence of God. I think that when Adam saw Eve fall, love overtook him. I think he said, "Why? Why did you do it? Now we can't be together." I'm convinced that Adam loved her so much that he ate of the fruit of the tree just to be able to continue to be with her. He gave himself up for her. Whether he thought that he was redeeming her or pitying her, we don't know. But he knew what he was doing. He committed idolatry by choosing the woman and not God. But God had a plan to redeem man.

Romans 5:6 For when we were still without strength, in due time Christ died for the ungodly.

"In due time" that plan came to pass. In God's timing, Christ's death on the cross came—not for the church-goers and the righteous—but for the ungodly. There were no godly people until that time. Everyone was "the ungodly."

Romans 5:7 For scarcely for a righteous man will one die; yet perhaps for a good man someone would even dare to die.

There are people who will put themselves in front of a bullet to protect the President of the United States. Agents of the Secret Service believe that it is better for the sake of the country that they die rather than the President. They are willing to sacrifice their lives for this good man.

What about the everyday heroes who we sometimes hear about, who risk their lives to rescue people in a burning building, or in a flood? The police force, firemen, and other rescue personnel are committed to giving themselves up for someone else. Even so, this is not a common event.

Romans 5:8-10 But God demonstrates His own love toward us, in that while we were *still sinners*, Christ died for us. Much more then, having now been justified by His blood, we shall be saved from wrath through Him. For if when we were enemies we were reconciled to God through the death of His Son, much more, having been reconciled, we shall be saved by His life. (Italics mine.)

Awesome Love

Imagine somebody you would consider to be the worst criminal in today's society. Think of a person who has committed grossly wicked crimes, maybe a mass-murderer. The person is caught, found guilty, and put in prison. Why did he do those horrible things? There's a demonic force in him that controlled him, and drove him to lust after blood and murder. I'm sure we would all agree, such an individual is society's enemy.

I remember when my wife, Linda, and I had our firstborn son. I remember everything. I remember the room Linda was in, the color of it, the sounds in it, and the discomfort she felt. I remember when the doctor said, "It's a boy."

Now, let's say my neighbor was that mass-murderer I mentioned. This man next door was going around killing children and eating their bodies. He was caught and now he's in prison. Let's say, I found out that if I would allow my son to die (after being brutally tortured) in place of my neighbor (the mass-murderer), he would be released from prison and be able to come back and live next door to me again.

My friend, I am in love with my son. I held him when he was only seconds old. I loved him the moment he was born, and have grown to love him even more as he's grown up. For me to say, "Okay, take my son. Beat and whip his back, torture him, and then execute him so that my neighbor can come live next door to me again," I'd better really love that man.

That man next door is **you and I**. We are the people who have worshiped another god. But God wants us to come back and live next door to Him again.

God loves you—individually—so much that He was willing to let Jesus go through the pain of being tortured and killed. Jesus was God's firstborn Son. God said, "Go ahead and torture Him, go ahead and murder Him, and then I'll take your sins and put them on Him." Is it no wonder that the sky went dark for three hours? Is it no wonder there was a cry in Jesus' being, "My God, My God, why have You forsaken Me?" I believe that God turned His face and had to weep.

God loves you so much that He willingly gave His only Son, because He wanted you to live next door to Him again. Jesus came to open up those prison doors to let us go free. Do you see how much He loves you?

Romans 5:9-10   Much more then, having now been justified by His blood, we shall be saved from wrath through Him. For if when we were enemies we were reconciled to God through the death of His Son, much more, having been reconciled, we shall be saved by His life.

Think about it. God looked at your life and you were behind the prison bars. You used to be His next door neighbor. He sent His Son to die for you, so you could come back to live next door to Him. Now you're reconciled to Him.

How Much More?

How much more does God love you now that you are redeemed? How much more is God willing to answer your prayers now that you are redeemed? How much more is God willing to help you now that you're His next door neighbor?

How much more? The Bible says, ". . . much more. . . by His life." (Romans 5:10)

CHAPTER 2

The Love of God in Action

There's a common definition of the word "grace" that is found in lexicons, concordances, and so forth. They say, "Grace: God's unmerited favor." That's probably what most of you think when you hear the word "grace." Most of us have heard that definition for years.

I would like for you to toss that definition out forever. The reason is because it declares "You're not worthy of God's favor. You don't deserve it, but God gives it to you anyway." This definition bothers me because God gave up His own Son! How dare we slap Him in the face by saying, "I'm not worthy?" God has said, "I've made you complete in Me. I have done a redemptive act, and now you **are** worthy of My grace."

Rather, let's understand grace with an easy definition: **the love of God in action**. God—through grace —redeemed man. How? He put His love in action. He didn't just love you, He did something about it. Today, by faith we stand in grace. (Romans 5:2)

Grace is God loving you and taking action by being involved in your life. We could say this equation:

Grace = God's Love in Action

For you to be able to love God, you must first know that God loves you. We must understand the relationship God wants us to have with Him. We must understand the relationship He made available to us, that is, forgiveness through the cross of Jesus Christ. When we can understand the depth of salvation, then we can understand the love of God.

Understanding All That Salvation Gives

I believe the number one problem with the adult world (13 years old and older) today is that they do not understand salvation. Oh, they may be born again, but they don't understand the scope of the salvation that was given to them.

We've preached the evangelical message for years "you must be born again." But have you ever examined the cross, and what God actually did for us? If we fully understand the completion of our deliverance, we will break the codependency on the things of the world, and come to complete dependency on the Spirit of God.

When we have this understanding, negative cycles will be broken, such as poverty, for instance. People caught in this vicious cycle seem never to be able to get ahead. They never have enough money for even the necessities in life.

People say, "yes," I'm born again; "yes," I'm going to heaven. If you ask people what they were delivered *from,* they would probably say they were delivered from hell. Well then, what were you delivered to? If you're delivered from something, then you must be delivered *to* something.

What did God give you in your salvation? Are you trying to earn it now? That's what most people are trying to do: earn their salvation. They're trying to merit what has been given to them.

Misunderstood Definitions

When we read the definition of grace being God's unmerited favor, we tell ourselves we don't deserve it, therefore, we end up trying to earn it. *Deserving and earning have absolutely nothing whatsoever to do with grace at all.*

What's the definition of sin? Now 95% of Christians will say "missing the mark." What mark? The mark of perfection? God didn't call us to perfection. He called us to a *relationship.*

And now we have a new generation of "Word" people. Do you know what is the major problem with Word people? They're trying to establish a relationship with the Word (Bible), instead of a relationship with God. That's where the problem lies.

We actually think that the more we read the Bible, the closer we'll be to Him. One day you've got to say, "I know Him." One day, you've got to look at God in His face and declare your personal love for Him. It simply paints a picture of Who God is and what He does for you in your life. The Bible merely shows you God.

Guess what? When we get to heaven, we're not going to need a Bible. We don't live in the Word, we live in God. Whatever I do, I do in Christ Jesus. ". . . the life which I now live in the flesh I live by faith in the Son of God, who loved me and gave Himself for me." (Galatians 2:20)

We live in a relationship with a Person called Father God. Yes, I believe wholeheartedly in studying the Bible regularly, and I believe in having devotions, but *we're not having a devotion with a Bible!* The Bible was given to me to show me the love of God. I'm not in love with the book, I'm in love with God.

Sometimes, in our private devotions, we think about how much we should be memorizing instead of how much we should be talking to God. It's very important to study the Bible and memorize verses, but let's not lose the focus of having a one-on-one relationship with Father God. God came to us through Jesus to have a personal relationship with us.

I John 4:7-8 Beloved, let us love one another, for love is of God; and everyone who loves is born of God and knows God. He who does not love does not know God, for God is love.

"Love one another" is an outward action. It tells us to do something. The ability to love one another comes from God. But so many people want to say, "God, will you love me now that I'm loving my brother?" You must understand that your love relationship with God will allow you to love your brother.

You can be born of God, but not be walking in your love relationship with God.

I John 4:9-11 In this the love of God was manifested toward us, that God has sent His only begotten Son into the world, that we might live through Him. In this is love, not that we loved God, but that He loved us and sent His Son to be the propitiation for our sins. Beloved, if God so loved us, we also ought to love one another.

We cannot love one another unless we understand the love God has for us personally. God always begins on the inside, and then an outward change occurs.

We need to take time to study the love of God: not how to love Him, but how much He loves us. There has been enough preaching about how God hates sin. I believe God hates sin. We don't need to be convinced to hate evil and live unto righteousness. We need to be told about God's love.

Romans 5:6-11 For when we were still without strength, in due time Christ died for the ungodly. For scarcely for a righteous man will one die; yet perhaps for a good man someone would even dare to die. But God demonstrates His own love toward us, in that while we were still sinners, Christ died for us. Much more then, having now been justified by His blood, we shall be saved from wrath through Him. For if when we were enemies we were reconciled to

God through the death of His Son, much more, having been reconciled, we shall be saved by His life. And not only that, but we also rejoice in God through our Lord Jesus Christ, through whom we have now received the reconciliation.

Love Letters

When I was in the military, I was sent to South Korea for 13 months. I thought I would not see my wife for that 13 months. But some things happened and I was able to bring her over six months later. During that separation, we wrote to each other every day. I "lived with my wife" through those letters. I read and reread those letters. I lived in them. I had a love relationship with her through those letters. But six months later, my wife came to Korea. When she was sitting in the room with me, I no longer needed to read her letters. I didn't need the letters anymore.

When Jesus returns, we won't need "the letters" anymore. In the meantime, we're reading His letters. While we read these letters, we love Jesus and have a relationship with Him. He wants to live His life through us as if He were here. During our lives on this earth, we're going to be reading His letters. We'll never get to the place here on earth where we don't need to read the letters. But we do want to get to the place that we are living the letters. We want to be "living epistles."

The Wrath of God

In the beginning, man had a love relationship with God. In Genesis 3, Adam fell from the presence of God which caused a big gap to be made between them. When man fell, he came under a curse. God cursed man which is the wrath of God. God's wrath is pointing to death, spiritual death. Spiritual death is separation from God. Death controlled man because of sin in his life. "The wages of sin is death." (Romans 6:23) Sin controls people who do not know God because they are dead, or separated, from God.

GOD

Death gives sin power to control man

On the day that Adam fell, God judged him as dead to Him. "You shall be eternally separated from Me." That is the wrath of God. The wrath of God comes unto man because of his spiritual death. Two things have taken place in man: he is separated from God, and he lives in sin.

GOD

God judges death with wrath

Sin is Forgiven

Now the cross comes in to redeem man. The first thing that happens is God puts all sin on Jesus. Before Jesus dies, He says, ". . . Father forgive them, for they do not know what they do." (Luke 23:34) God the Father then forgives all sin: past, present, and future. Sin is no longer an issue. It is taken away through Jesus Christ. God forgave sin.

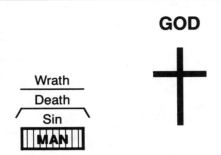

GOD

Wrath

Death

Sin

MAN

God puts sin on the cross

Forgiven People Go To Hell

People whose sins were forgiven go to hell every day. What? Yes, the way to heaven is not to have your sins forgiven, it is to be born again. (This is not false doctrine. Don't stop reading, just read carefully and understand.)

Everybody's sins have been forgiven. Even Hitler's sins were put on the cross of Jesus Christ. He was a forgiven person who went to hell. Every person who's died and gone to hell had their sins already forgiven.

Having your sins forgiven is not the way to heaven. You must be born again to go to heaven because that way, you become alive to God. The sins of the whole world were forgiven when Jesus died on the cross.

Behavior Gospel

What is the Church preaching today? The Church is preaching sin. The Church of the United States is preaching a morality gospel. It is preaching a works and behavior gospel instead of a gospel of life.

We have a living relationship with God, not a behavior relationship. When our relationship with God is right, then our behavior will be right.

People are dying inside. People are going to therapy because inside they think they're no good. Outwardly, they're not sinning, outwardly they're not committing adultery, outwardly they're not looking at pornography, but inwardly, these good people are decaying like a bad tooth that is rotting away on the inside.

The Church is falling apart on the inside. Why? Because inside, Christians don't think they're good people. They've been convinced that they're "no good, rotten sinners just barely saved by grace."

The reason people fall into codependency, low self-esteem, and mental problems is because they don't understand the love of God and the way He works in them. God wants to work from the inside out. But because of what has been preached to them about sin, a lot of Christians are attempting to conform outwardly in their own strength.

Quit preaching sin, and start preaching life! Sin has been forgiven. Jesus Christ took care of it. Paul says, "You that sin, sin no more." Well wait, don't I need to go to 25 weeks of support groups? No, just stop sinning. I'm not against support groups (we have several in our own church), but if all of us preachers had been teaching the gospel of grace and the power of God, we wouldn't need them. The *power* is the *love* of God.

What is the Problem?

Sin is no longer a problem to God. God has taken care of it by placing it on Jesus on the cross. God *has* forgiven the world of their sins. But sin was not the problem in the first place. Sin is a product of spiritual death. Spiritual death is separation from God. God has judged death with His wrath. God's wrath is on people who are dead to Him: people who have never been born again. You go to hell because you have rejected *life,* not because you have unforgiven sins.

Now to those who have been born again, the question is this: "What am I delivered to? What is my salvation?"

- For death, He has given us life.
- For sin, He has given us righteousness.
- For wrath, He has given us peace.

God has not called you to His wrath. We are the redeemed.

God has called us to His family. Wrath is over death. Death gets its power from sin. I am now born again.

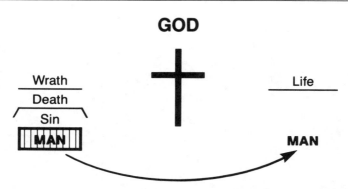

The person who is born again is removed from death and given life in Jesus. There is NO wrath over him.

When a person says "yes" to Jesus, they become born again. They are removed from the death of man to the life of God. Instead of death, God gives them life. They are also removed from the wrath of God because they are no longer dead to God. Since they are alive to God, they have peace with Him. Instead of wrath, He has given us peace. All of this is by grace and not works.

> **Ephesians 2:8-10   For by grace you have been saved through faith, and that not of yourselves; it is the gift of God, not of works, lest anyone should boast. For we are His workmanship, created in Christ Jesus for good works, which God prepared beforehand that we should walk in them.**

What have you been saved from? Most people think they have been saved from sin. No, we've been saved from the wrath of God. When you were born again, you were born from the dead and made alive to God. When you're made alive to God, you're saved from the wrath of God. People who are dead to God, go to a place called hell. Hell, at the end of the world, gets thrown into the Lake of Fire. In the Lake of Fire, those people are eternally damned.

CHAPTER 3

Can God Love Me?

John 3:16 says, "For God so loved the world that He gave His only begotten Son . . ." Let's focus on *you* as a part of "the world." We could even say, "God so loved *me*, that He gave His only begotten Son . . ."

What is the purpose of reading my Bible? What is the purpose of having daily devotions? Why study? Why do I do these things? Because I want a relationship—a one-on-one relationship—with the Father.

Our goal is not to memorize Bible verses; our goal is to have a relationship with Father God. The way to reach a goal is to have strategies. You can't *do* a goal, you can only accomplish it. You set a goal, but you do strategies. A strategy leads you to the goal.

Some of those strategies would be reading my Bible, studying my Bible and other reference books, memorizing scripture, having prayer time, going to church, participating in worship services, listening to tapes, etc. As Christians we use these strategies to reach the goal of a strong relationship with the Father.

Jesus introduced God as "Father God" to the people of His day. Do we feel that strong in our relationship so that we can go to other people and do the same thing?

Performance v. Relationship

In the United States, the majority of us have heard a gospel of works and performance, not one of relationship. When we live the gospel of relationship, good actions will result from it.

When a man and woman meet, they don't **know** each other after the first date. It takes time to get to know each other. A relationship develops, causing the couple to be faithful to each other because of love.

After marriage, the ability to resist temptation and the lust of the flesh comes from the strength of the love you have inside your heart for God. I study the Bible, not to conform to the image God wants me to be, but because I'm in love with Jesus. Because I'm in love with Him, I won't want to offend Him; I won't want to sin against Him. So conformity comes out of love, not love out of conformity.

If we can develop our own personal love for God, then we'll have more strength to resist the lust of the world and walk through life in victory. God first loved us, so we could love Him (I John 4:9-12). I cannot release my love for God until I know how much He loves me.

All deliverance is based upon your acceptance of God's love for you personally. If you need deliverance or freedom from a tragedy you have had in your life, you must first gain a revelation of God's love for you personally.

If you don't, you can only "act like" or conform to a delivered lifestyle, but not have one. We have a lot of Christians who outwardly conform to a certain lifestyle, but inside, they need a "root canal."

Understanding Salvation

After man fell from God, there was nothing he could do by himself to get back into a righteous relationship with God. Can you be good enough to get saved? Can you give enough money to the Church to get saved? Can you pray enough to get saved? Can you go to church long enough to get saved? Can you be a 90-year old grandmother who bakes pies for all the neighbors and never gets angry at anyone to get saved? No! Man cannot become good enough to earn his way into heaven. Jesus said, ". . . No one comes to the Father except through Me." (John 14:6)

When Jesus died on the cross, He was the sacrifice that paid the price for our sin. He asked, "Father, forgive them, for they do not know what they do." (Luke 23:34) He wasn't just talking about the Roman soldiers at His feet but the sin of the whole world.

The Resurrection

Did you know that if Jesus had stayed in the grave, sin would still have been taken care of, but we would still have "death"? God had to raise Jesus from the dead, so that we could receive His life in us and be born again. You don't go to heaven because your sins are forgiven. You go to heaven because you are born again. In John 3:3, Jesus did not say to Nicodemus, "You must have your sins forgiven," He said, ". . . unless one is born again, he cannot see the kingdom of God."

It's the blood of Jesus Christ on the mercy seat in heaven in the Holy of Holies, that eradicates the wrath of God. We are not appointed to wrath.

Can God love me? Sure He can because death is completely removed when you were born again! The blood of Jesus has removed the wrath of God from our lives because we are no longer dead to God but alive.

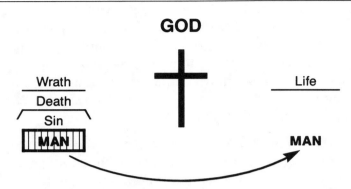

The person who is born again is removed from death and given life in Jesus. There is NO wrath over him.

Key Scripture

> **Romans 5:6-10** **For when we were still without strength, in due time Christ died for the ungodly. For scarcely for a righteous man will one die; yet perhaps for a good man someone would even dare to die.** *But God demonstrates His own love toward us, in that while we were still sinners, Christ died for us.* **Much more then, having now been justified by His blood, we shall be saved from wrath through Him. For if when we were enemies we were reconciled to God through the death of His Son, much more, having been reconciled, we shall be saved by His life.** (Italics mine.)

You've been appointed to the blessings of God, not the wrath of God, which leaves you in a right relationship with God the Father. Does that mean that you'll never sin, or make a mistake again? No, it means that you can commune with God; you can have the power of the Spirit in your life; you can make some significant changes in your life. Why? Because God loves you *personally.*

Righteousness does not mean perfection, it means a right thing has happened: a righteous act. God takes something that was wrong and makes it right. God gives us an opportunity to grow, and allows us to make mistakes. He cuts us some slack, some space.

People need to know God loves them. You might say, "Pastor, you don't understand, just last night I committed a big sin." I'm certainly not condoning sexual sin, drug addiction, or any other sin. What I'm trying to help you begin to understand is if God loves you so much that He sent His Son to die for you, then He *will* surely help you with any weakness in your life.

Romans 8:32   He who did not spare His own Son, but delivered Him up for us all, how shall He not with Him also freely give us all things?

God wants to work *inside* of you today. If you would simply confess an area of weakness in your life and say, "God, I need you to help me walk through this, and get this out of my life," He will begin a process of deliverance. He will work on the inside of you to get that evil, fleshly thing out for good.

But so many people in church are so self-righteous that they have no place in their church for people who need space to grow in Christ. They just want to "get them out of the church." They look down at people with sin problems and think they shouldn't be in church. That's where they're supposed to be! Church is supposed to filled with prostitutes, drug addicts, pimps, AIDS victims, homosexuals, and lesbians! That's what the church is for!

A church is a place for restoring people to a right relationship with God. It's not supposed to be full of perfect people. Church is full of people who have needs. If God's going to let people grow, why can't we?

Ephesians 2:8-10   For by grace you have been saved through faith, and that not of yourselves; it is the gift of God, not of works, lest anyone should boast. For we are His workmanship, created in Christ Jesus for *good works*, which God prepared beforehand that we should walk in them. (Italics mine.)

In Christianity, the good works that God has called you to do are a part of living as a Christian. You're not a Christian because you do good works. Good works come out of your *relationship with God.*

In your life, there will be temptations that will come to challenge you. When that happens, be careful not to close your life down and say, "Oh no, I guess all those good works I've done in the past don't count now because look at this horrible desire I have." You start to judge yourself because of the theology you've been taught and think "I guess I must not have ever been saved, because if I was saved, that thought would never have entered my mind."

No! Even the people preaching that don't believe it. Every single person has evil works within them. The good news is that God wants to help us change!

God says Christianity is a progressive lifestyle that can go in both directions. If you give yourself over to lawlessness, it will grow. If you give yourself over to righteousness, it too, will grow and grow.

God absolutely knows that when we start our Christian walk, sin diminishes if we develop righteousness. God realizes that until we're gone from this earth, there will be sin in our lives. Why are we so wrapped up in the *actions of our flesh instead of the attitude of our hearts*?

The Father looks at our lives and says, "Jesus has died for you. You are My sons and you are My daughters. Awake unto righteousness, and sin not! Awake to the relationship you have in Me. Understand that I love you!"

When we develop a love for God, there will be power to break sin and the weakness of the flesh in us. There will be a conformity—an agreeing—with the work that is on the inside of us. We'll be "working out our own salvation" from the inside out.

You'll be a powerful believer when you know "My God has delivered me already!" Remember, obedience is from the heart, not the body.

I was talking to a man once who firmly believed that every sin had to be confessed or it wasn't forgiven, and therefore the person would go to hell. I challenged him by asking what if he got into a fight with his wife, rushed out of the house, slammed the door, jumped in the car, drove down the street and got into an accident and was killed. You didn't have time to confess the sin of anger. Would you go to hell? His answer was "Yes." That's sad. Someone did not tell him the truth.

You don't go to heaven because you have no sin. You go to heaven because you're *alive to God*. You go to *hell* because you're *dead to God*.

CHAPTER 4

Righteousness: A Two-Way Relationship

The word righteousness is used many times in the Bible to explain our relationship with God. Many people, when when they hear the word righteousness, think of a right performance for God instead of how the Bible uses it: a right relationship with God.

We need to see righteousness as a two-way relationship with God and man. From God to man, it is God making right what was wrong; from man to God, it is man relating to God in his new life.

Righteousness is a relational term, not a performance term. God wants man to be with Him so God made what was wrong with man, right. This was an act of righteousness from God to man. Man wants to relate back with God and be in this relationship, right-standing, or right-relating to Him. Therefore, man relates to God on the terms that God has said is right.

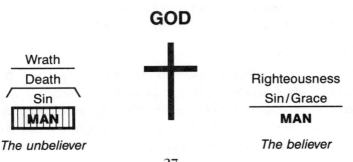

GOD

The unbeliever		The believer
Wrath		Righteousness
Death		Sin/Grace
Sin		MAN
MAN		

When Adam committed sin against God, it resulted in his spiritual death. This is separation from God. Adam's death has given sin its power to control man from that day forward. God judged death with wrath, so the outcome is that all will be sent to hell because of their death toward God. They have no relationship with God.

Let me explain to you where we are going with this. You need to know about four very important chapters in the book of Romans: chapters 5, 6, 7, and 8. The subjects of these chapters are the following:

- **Romans 5: Explains salvation.**
- **Romans 6: A Christian living under the control of sin.** To whatever you submit yourself, you become a slave to it, whether sin unto death, or righteousness unto life.
- **Romans 7: A Christian living under the law.** You really want to do right, but every time you try to do right, you do wrong.
- **Romans 8: A Christian living by the Spirit.** When your mind is stayed on the Lord, when you walk in the Spirit, when you are spiritually-minded, you are living the Spirit-led life.

We want to be Romans 8 Christians. However, everybody goes through the steps of Romans 5, 6, and 7 first.

> **Romans 5:12   Therefore, just as through one man [Adam] sin entered the world, and death through sin, and thus death spread [not sin] to all men, because all sinned [the sin of Adam]. . .** (Brackets mine.)

Two Deaths

Spiritual death is separation from God. Spiritual death leads to physical death. When God created Adam and Eve, no one was ever supposed to die. We were not created to die physically, but we do die physically because of the death that came in from Adam's sin. Death comes to everyone because of him.

Everyone is either dead to God, or alive to God. The born-again experience is going from death to life. The reason a person who is morally good and right (but not born again) still goes to hell, is because they are dead to God. Remember, it is not the abstaining from sin that gets you to heaven.

Romans 5:13   For until the law sin was in the world, but sin is not imputed when there is no law.

Before the law came, God did not even address the sin issue.

Romans 5:14   Nevertheless death reigned from Adam to Moses, even over those who had not sinned according to the likeness of the transgression of Adam, who is a type of Him who was to come.

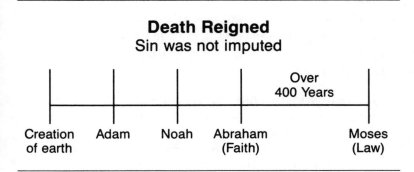

Death Reigned
Sin was not imputed

| | | | Over 400 Years | |
| Creation of earth | Adam | Noah | Abraham (Faith) | Moses (Law) |

Abraham is called the father of faith. He lived and died over 400 years before God ever gave the law. Sin entered the world with Adam. Abraham shows us an example of living by faith.

God said He wouldn't even consider the subject of sin at that time. He didn't even impute sin because there was no law. If there's no law to tell you you're doing something wrong, you don't know you're sinning.

Yet all the people who lived and died from Adam to Moses who did not look for the redemption to come, went to hell. God, in Genesis 3, tells Adam and Eve that the seed of the woman was going to redeem them. Adam and Eve taught the redemption plan to their children.

Then you will ask, "If God did not impute sin, why would all of those people go to hell if they didn't believe in the redemption?" Because they were dead to God. Only the people who looked for the promised redemption were alive to God. These were the people who were living by faith. (Hebrews 11:39, 40)

You can see from Romans 5:14 that even though God did not impute sin, death still reigned. Death reigned over all of those people. God was working on the life issue, not on the sin issue. When the law was written, God began working on the sin issue.

Did Noah go to heaven? Yes. Did Abraham go to heaven? Yes. When Adam was created, God introduced life. Through Abraham, God introduced faith. Through Moses, God introduced the law, and the law introduced sin. God talked about faith first, then about sin.

Romans 5:15-18   But the free gift is not like the offense. For if by the one man's offense [Adam] many died, much more the grace of God and the gift by the grace of the one Man, Jesus Christ, abounded to many. And the gift is not like that which came through the one who sinned. For the judgment which came from one offense resulted in condemnation, but the free gift which came from many offenses resulted in justification. For if by the one man's offense death reigned through the one, much more those who receive abundance of grace and of the gift of righteousness will reign in life through the One, Jesus Christ. Therefore, as through one man's offense judgment came to all men, resulting in condemnation, even so through one Man's righteous act the free gift came to all men, resulting in justification of life. (Brackets mine.)

The gift of grace is salvation where death is eradicated. You are not a sinner saved by grace! You were dead in your sins, and you've been made alive by Jesus Christ. There are no sinners in heaven. Remember, sin isn't the issue, it's death and life. God is redeeming people from death to life. "You must be born again." Remember, everybody's sins were forgiven at the cross of Christ.

Anyone who calls on the name of the Lord shall be saved. Death is then removed and I have life controlling me. When my flesh lusts against my spirit, my spirit now has more authority over my actions. Why? Because I have the Holy Spirit controlling my life with power over sin through Jesus Christ!

Why the Law?

Why then was the law given at all? One reason is to expose sin. The law shows us we have sin. That is still true today. It shows me weaknesses in my life.

God wants you to know that He has not called you to a life of sinlessness. He's called you to a life of walking in the Spirit, being empowered by the Spirit, and saying "no" to the evil powers of this world. Overcoming sin and lust in this world is accomplished by His Spirit and His grace, not by our works of righteousness.

> **Romans 5:20-21 Moreover the law entered that the offense might abound. But where sin abounded, grace abounded much more, so that as sin reigned in death, even so grace might reign through righteousness to eternal life through Jesus Christ our Lord.**

The word "entered" is a theatrical term for a secondary actor who takes a step back when the star, or primary actor, comes on stage. That primary actor is "grace." Grace is introduced by Jesus Christ and after He is resurrected, He leaves grace here.

The law was designed by God to show how sinful we were. It was brought into man's life to show him his weaknesses, to conform to God in order to be approved and receive life from God. The law will show you your problems. It was designed to arouse the passions of sin that are in your flesh.

I'd like to show you more clearly what takes place: The law enters to show you that you are dead to God. You also discover that you have an uncontrolled physical body called "the flesh." The law brings to light your weakness to God. Therefore, you cannot become born again by the law. The law was sent to bring you to salvation. Instead, it reveals your "deadness" to God.

Performance Christianity

Let me ask you a question. Whatever your church background, have you been under the belief that you were never to do one wrong act, never have one wrong thought? Do you believe that you should go to bed at night knowing that you did absolutely everything God wanted you to do?

I've thought this way, particularly because of the definition of "holiness," that God wanted perfect conformity to an outward lifestyle, and if I wasn't perfect, I disappointed Him. I was also indoctrinated to believe that if I did sin, God maybe even hated me.

If that were the truth, it would be the ultimate abuse of God's Word. If God's will was for us to be perfect, why did He establish grace? Grace says that even if I can't perform the law, I'm accepted because of the Beloved. God wants me to realize my absolute dependency on the Holy Spirit. Wouldn't it be reasonable then to say, if I could perform perfectly for the Lord, why would I need the Holy Spirit?

"Okay, my sins are all forgiven. So then, should I just go ahead and continue in sin?" Paul says strongly in Romans 6:2, absolutely not, are you fools?

Grace is strengthened by relationship. The more grace, the more sin gets pushed out of our lives. Just as in the relationship of marriage, a wife doesn't want her husband to just buy her flowers and candy and never spend time with her. She wants her husband to spend time, sit with her face to face and talk with her, in order to build their relationship. God, too, wants us to sit down with Him and talk face to face! He doesn't want you to just pray for other people, just give money and time to your church—He wants you to know Him.

I used to be one who thought I had to perform correctly in order to receive grace from God. I lived in a way that said I had to perform a certain way to get forgiveness and blessings. I have found that God wants me to develop my relationship with Him, and then His grace is increased. I am to be dependent on the Holy Spirit.

What we have is a war between our spirit and our flesh. If we live in this right relationship with God, grace will abound; if we refuse to communicate through this relationship with God, sin will abound. Sin is designed to do one thing: pull you from God and His blessings.

Submission to God is a submission to His orders in our lives. His orders are not to get us to perform or to gain His approval, but rather, for grace to abound and His blessings to also abound in our lives.

CHAPTER 5

He Took It All Away

Romans 5:17   For if by the one man's offense *death reigned* through the one, much more those who receive abundance of grace and of the gift of righteousness will reign in life through the One, Jesus Christ. (Italics mine.)

Romans 5:20-21   Moreover the law entered that the offense might abound. But where sin abounded, grace abounded much more, so that as *sin reigned in death*, even so grace might reign through righteousness to eternal life through Jesus Christ our Lord. (Italics mine.)

Man, in his fallen state, is being controlled by sin. Sin gets its control from death. Man, who is not a believer in God, is in relationship with death. He is dead to God. He is not alive to God.

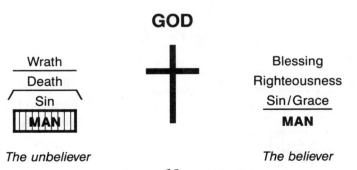

GOD

Wrath	Blessing
Death	Righteousness
Sin	Sin / Grace
MAN	**MAN**
The unbeliever	*The believer*

As we can see, the unbeliever is being controlled by death which gives power to sin. The believer is being controlled by righteousness which is his right relationship with God. This relationship gives power to grace which is controlling the man's life. Grace reigns through righteousness or through the relationship that man has with God. Therefore, if the man develops his relationship—improves or matures in it—there will be more grace controlling his life.

God has two relationships. He has a relationship with the unbeliever and He has a relationship with the believer.

- **Relationship with unbelievers.**
  This is the wrath side of God. Those who are not believers are being controlled by sin. Man is imprisoned by sin. God has placed His wrath on sin. Unbelievers are dead to God.

- **Relationship with believers.**
  This is the blessing side of God. Believers have life with God because of the removal of wrath. The cross of Christ brings man to spiritual life with God. However, within man's flesh there is still sin because "this corruptible must put on incorruption." But where sin abounds, grace abounds much more. Believers are alive to God or in a righteousness relationship.

The Bible says "God is love." There are two sides to the love of God: the "yes" side and the "no" side.

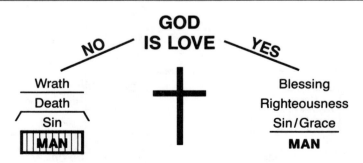

Two sides to the love of God

God's love says "no" to death, a dead relationship to God. God keeps His wrath on this side. But we (believers) are not appointed to wrath.

Romans 5:21 ...so that as sin reigned in death, even so grace might reign through righteousness to eternal life through Jesus Christ our Lord.

God's love says "yes" to life: an alive relationship with God. God's "yes" side gives blessing and righteousness. Grace reigns through righteousness.

We will no longer be controlled by sin if we will give ourselves over to a relationship with God. **The more we develop our personal relationship with the Father, the Son, and the Holy Spirit, the more grace is poured out in our lives.**

Can Christians Sin?

At the cross our sins were forgiven. Because we are born again, we are delivered from death. However, our flesh has not yet been delivered from the *ability to sin*.

Romans 5:20 Moreover the law entered that the offense might abound. But where sin abounded, grace abounded much more...

Have you sinned since you were born again? Of course, the answer is "yes." Whether Christians sin really isn't the issue. The issue is are we going to be controlled by grace? For where sin abounds, grace does **much more** abound in a righteousness relationship.

Well, if grace abounds much more where sin abounds, then why should I stop sinning? You need to understand that grace will not abound if you give yourself over to sin. It abounds when you give yourself over to righteousness.

When a person is developing their relationship with God, grace abounds but not through works.

Romans 6:1, 2, 7-9   What shall we say then? Shall we continue in sin that grace may abound? Certainly not! How shall we who died to sin live any longer in it? For he who has died has been freed from sin. Now if we died with Christ, we believe that we shall also live with Him, knowing that Christ, having been raised from the dead, dies no more. Death no longer has dominion over Him.

When you look at your life and see sin, you must look at yourself through the eyes of grace. You must see that you're alive to God and the control of sin has been broken. Don't look at the law, compute your sin, and think how awful you are.

We must constantly be looking at what Christ has done in our lives. There is sin because we have flesh, and our flesh has not been changed yet.

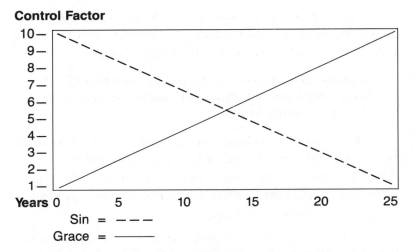

Control Factor

Sin = – – –
Grace = ———

1—10 is the control factor in your life. It shows the control of sin or grace.
0—25 are the years after you are born again. The chart displays the growth in Christ we gain in grace and lose in sin.

Romans 6:12   Therefore do not let sin reign in your mortal body. . .

When sin shows up in your life, deal with it through the power of grace. Don't tell God, "I'll prove it to you, God. In ten days I won't do that act."

If you are a Christian living your life with the "don't" word (don't do this, don't say that), your life is consumed and controlled by sin. Sin is reigning in your life even if you're not committing sin. You're living your relationship with God by what you don't do. That's called pride.

Instead, relate with God. When sin shows up, deal with it through God's grace. Realize you've been forgiven, then submit to the chastisement of the Lord.

Romans 6:13-14   And do not present your members as instruments of unrighteousness to sin, but present yourselves to God as being alive from the dead, and your members as instruments of righteousness to God. For sin shall not have dominion over you, for you are not under law but under grace.

As soon as you put yourself under the law—performance Christianity—to prove you are righteous, you will have sin in control of your life. Instead, move under grace. First, you've got to submit to a relationship with God, then as you develop that relationship, grace will abound. The sin in your life will start to die and have no dominion.

CHAPTER 6

Submission v. Chastisement

Believers: Awake and Asleep

I Thessalonians 5:1-10 But concerning the times and the seasons, brethren, you have no need that I should write to you. For you yourselves know perfectly that the day of the Lord so comes as a thief in the night. For when they say, 'Peace and safety!'' then sudden destruction comes upon them, as labor pains upon a pregnant woman. And they shall not escape. But you, brethren, are not in darkness, so that this Day should overtake you as a thief. You are all sons of light and sons of the day. We are not of the night nor of darkness. Therefore let us not sleep, as others do, but let us watch and be sober. For those who sleep, sleep at night, and those who get drunk are drunk at night. But let us who are of the day be sober, putting on the breastplate of faith and love, and as a helmet the hope of salvation. *For God did not appoint us to wrath,* but to obtain salvation through our Lord Jesus Christ, who died for us, that whether we wake or sleep, we should live together with Him. (Italics mine.)

Paul introduces something to us in this chapter. We have two categories of believers: those who are awake and those who are asleep.

We've probably all heard the teaching that when the rapture comes, only the "awake" believers go up. What about verse 10? ". . .whether we wake or sleep, we should live together with Him."

Now the question arises, if all the people who sleep still get to be with Jesus in heaven, why should we stop sinning since we are no longer under the law?

Paul was asked this question after his teaching on grace.

Romans 6:15 What then? Shall we sin because we are not under law but under grace? Certainly not!

God is not dealing with sin in your life by the law. He is dealing with sin in your life by grace. A believer has the ability to sin. (Christians can sin as well as anyone!) However, it has nothing to do with your relationship with God in the sense of life and death.

What happens to those Christians who want to continue to sin?

As I mentioned before, there is a "yes" and a "no" side to God's love. On the "yes" side of God's love, there are two sides of righteousness: the submission side and the chastisement side.

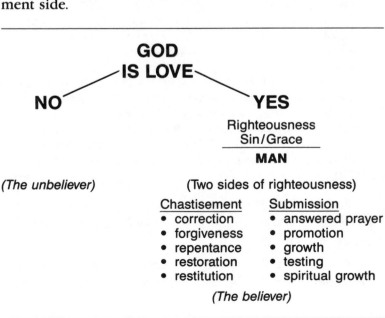

GOD IS LOVE

NO   **YES**

Righteousness
Sin / Grace
MAN

(The unbeliever)   *(Two sides of righteousness)*

Chastisement	Submission
• correction	• answered prayer
• forgiveness	• promotion
• repentance	• growth
• restoration	• testing
• restitution	• spiritual growth

(The believer)

The submission side of righteousness includes these areas:

- answered prayer
- promotion
- growth
- testing
- spiritual growth (II Peter 1)

The believer who submits to this side, will have all of these things added to their lives. The believer who lives in submission will be exalted in the kingdom of God.

James 4:10 "Humble yourselves in the sight of the Lord, and He will lift you up."

The chastisement side of righteousness includes these areas:

- correction
- forgiveness
- repentance
- restoration
- restitution

The believer who is not submitting to God and wants to continue to sin will be chastised. The whole purpose of chastisement is to produce submission. When you face something in life, you can choose the road of chastisement or the road of submission. It's your choice.

Chastisement is not punishment, it is correction. As with little children, correction through instruction and spankings leads to the right behavior.

Unbelievers see the wrath of God. Believers see the chastisement of God. Even believers who are sinning do not see the wrath of God.

For example, my wife and I are at a mall and she decides to go out to the car ahead of me. I approach the car and see that a man is attacking her. He's going to see my wrath! He's not going to see my chastisement. It's a totally different kind of relationship.

I Corinthians 15:34 says, "Awake to righteousness, and do not sin . . ."

Why not awake to God's greatest blessings, submit to His Word and His will, and not choose to take the road of hard knocks?

Hebrews 12:1, 2   Therefore we also, since we are surrounded by so great a cloud of witnesses, let us lay aside every weight, and *the sin which so easily ensnares us,* and let us run with endurance the race that is set before us, looking unto Jesus, the author and finisher of our faith, who for the joy that was set before Him endured the cross, despising the shame, and has sat down at the right hand of the throne of God. (Italics mine.)

Did you know that every single person has one major area of weakness which can be their ". . . sin which so easily ensnares . . ."?

Hebrews 12:5-10   And you have forgotten the exhortation which speaks to you as to sons: "My son, do not despise the chastening of the LORD, Nor be discouraged when you are rebuked by Him; For whom the LORD loves He chastens, And scourges every son whom He receives." If you endure chastening, God deals with you as with sons; for what son is there whom a father does not chasten? But if you are without chastening, of which all have become partakers, then you are illegitimate and not sons. Furthermore, we have had human fathers who corrected us, and we paid them respect. Shall we not much more readily be in subjection to the Father of spirits and live? For they indeed for a few days chastened us as seemed best to them, but He for our profit, that we may be partakers of His holiness.

We've been taught for many years that sin is the whole issue of Christianity, so all Christians should stop sinning.

Remember, sin is not the issue because Christ bore our sins on the cross. The issue is developing our relationship with God the Father in a more intimate way.

Let's take, for example, several prominent preachers who, in the last few years, have been widely publicized for their weaknesses and sins. During the many years of their respective ministries, they participated in habitual sexual, alcoholic, and drug addiction sins. Yet, all throughout those same years, they led thousands and thousands of people to salvation and healing.

How can this be? Something tells me that my former theology isn't right. That theology says if you have any kind of secret sin you are less than a Christian, even to the point that God hates you. You must perform in a certain lifestyle in order to stay accepted in the eyes of God. In a nutshell, this theology says, "Sin in your life equals God out of your life. Sin means no results in your ministry." If you believe that but start seeing results again and again, one day you start to believe "What I'm doing must not be sin afterall." At that point, you become sin's slave. The sin will control you. If you don't submit to the chastisement of God, your sin will find you out.

I am convinced that every one of those ministers mentioned above are Christians and they really love Jesus. The problem is they are in bondage to their flesh. They have all cried and cried, begging God for their deliverance. But here is the amazing truth: God looks at the obedience of the heart. If those ministers had known that truth, events would not have happened as they did.

The purpose of chastisement is not exaltation. It is to get the person to submit. Through that submission, the believer will learn how to grow spiritually, walk through testing, and receive promotion. Chastisement is a training time. It's not designed to promote you, but to get you to submit to God's Word.

Hebrews 12:11   Now no chastening seems to be joyful for the present, but painful; nevertheless, afterward it yields the peaceable fruit of righteousness to those who have been trained by it.

When you submit to God then you will be tested. Testing is on the submission side, not the chastisement side. When Abraham submitted himself to God, God tested him. When Moses submitted to God, God tested him. When Paul submitted to God, God tested him.

The testing comes after the submission. When you submit and say, "Okay, I'm ready to go," then God tests your faith.

Hebrews 12:12-17   Therefore strengthen the hands which hang down, and the feeble knees, and make straight paths for your feet, so that what is lame may not be dislocated, but rather be healed. Pursue peace with all people, and holiness, without which no one will see the Lord: looking carefully lest anyone fall short of the grace of God; lest any root of bitterness springing up cause trouble, and by this many become defiled; lest there be any fornicator or profane person like Esau, who for one morsel of food sold his birthright. For you know that afterward, when he wanted to inherit the blessing, he was rejected, for he found no place for repentance, though he sought it diligently with tears.

A person who continues to submit to their sin life becomes a slave to that sin. When a person chooses that route and refuses to submit to God's chastisement, grace is not reigning because sin has taken over. But when something tragic happens in that individual's life, then he or she wants all this faith to believe God for deliverance from it. But because of the lack of submission to God, the faith needed isn't there.

There is no reason for sin to control your life when grace has the right to control your life. But when you continue purposely to say "yes" to sin and "no" to God, you're selling out your birthright.

God Will Test You

As we have learned, there are two sides to righteousness. One is the submission side, the other is the chastisement side. We would like to avoid chastisement, so we must continually do what James 4:10 tells us. "Humble yourselves in the sight of the Lord, and He will lift you up."

Submission will always lead to testing. In the testing that God brings into your life, He will expose weaknesses so they can, in turn, be changed into strengths.

Every person has weaknesses because of our frail human nature. Those weaknesses are not all the same. What is a particular weakness to one person, is not to another. People have different weaknesses.

God intends for us to go through certain experiences in order to expose our weaknesses. He wants us to admit that these are our areas of weakness, then submit them to God. If we do this, we will grow and be exalted in due time.

To illustrate how our weaknesses are exposed so we can develop in spiritual maturity, picture a metal pipe. Let's say it's an oil pipeline in Alaska. The engineers take a section of the pipe before it's put in the ground to test it.

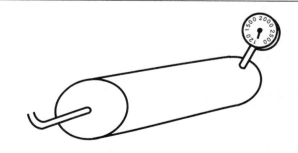

They cap it off at both ends and put a gauge on it to see how many pounds per square inch it can handle. Let's say they want it to be able to have 2,200 psi. They start pumping in water until it gets up to 1,600 and it suddenly springs a leak. They drain the water out, patch up the leak, then fill it up again. Then it gets to 1,800 psi.

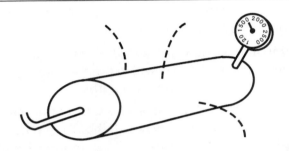

They continue the process until there are no leaks at 2,200 psi. The testing of the pipe did not create the leaks. It exposed the weakness that was already there.

When you submit to God and are tested, you're going to spring a leak. The purpose of springing a leak is so God can show you a weakness that was already there. Your husband, your children, your neighbor, your neighbor's dog, did not cause your leak. It was already there. When the testing comes, we need to deal with the leak (our area of weakness). If we don't deal with the weakness, when we hit the 2,200 psi later on, other leaks will show up and we'll be out of control. God wants you to deal with it now, because later on in life it will be too much to deal with. If we deal with it, we don't have to cross over to the chastisement side of righteousness.

CHAPTER 7

Relationship by Faith, Not Works

The Holy Spirit has come into the world to do two things: convict the world, and lead the Christian in righteousness.

The Holy Spirit's relationship with the unbeliever is one of conviction. The unbeliever is on the "no" side of God's righteousness.

> **John 16:5-9** "But now I go away to Him who sent Me, and none of you asks Me, 'Where are You going?' But because I have said these things to you, sorrow has filled your heart. Nevertheless I tell you the truth. It is to your advantage that I go away; for if I do not go away, the Helper will not come to you; but if I depart, I will send Him to you. And when He has come, *He will convict the world of sin,* and of righteousness, and of judgment; of sin, *because they do not believe in Me. . .*" (Italics mine.)

The Holy Spirit convicts the world of the sin of not believing in Jesus Christ. He doesn't convict them of being adulterers, liars, or murderers. What good does it do for an unbeliever to stop sinning if they are dead to God?

First, the Holy Spirit's conviction of sin to the unbeliever says, "You are dead to God, but you can become alive and be a part of the family of God." The sin is unbelief, that is, not believing in Christ.

We do not need to be telling unbelievers what the Holy Spirit is already telling them. We need to be telling them about the answer: Jesus Christ. We need to tell them the good news of life in Jesus, not what rotten sinners they are.

John 16:10 ". . .of righteousness, because I go to My Father and you see Me no more. . ."

Secondly, the Holy Spirit convicts the unbeliever of unrighteousness. Righteousness is a right relationship with God. The unbeliever has a wrong relationship with God.

John 16:11 ". . .of judgment, because the ruler of this world is judged."

Thirdly, the Holy Spirit convicts the unbeliever of judgment because the ruler of this world is judged. This is the wrath of God.

The Holy Spirit convicts unbelievers in the three following areas:
- Sin
- Righteousness
- Judgment

Nowhere in the Bible does it say that the Holy Spirit convicts the *believer* of righteousness and judgment.

The Holy Spirit **leads** the believer in grace through righteousness. The only conviction of sin that the Holy Spirit leads the believer in is on the chastisement side. He leads the believer to the deliverance of a weakness that is in their flesh.

We are the righteousness of God. We're not appointed to the wrath of God; therefore, when a sin is revealed, it is to lead us out of that sin.

The Prodigal Son

Luke 15 describes two believers. One of them wants to continue in sin, and the other wants to live under the law.

Luke 15:11-13   Then He said: "A certain man had two sons. And the younger of them said to his father, 'Father, give me that portion of goods that falls to me.' So he divided to them his livelihood. And not many days after, the younger son gathered all together, journeyed to a far country, and there wasted his possessions with prodigal [sinful] living." (Brackets mine.)

The first son is living in sin, but the second son is trying to gain approval by law: works. Most people look at the first son, but let's look carefully at both of them.

In the story of the prodigal son, the first son is not willing to submit to the father's plan. He wants to continue in his lust. The father recognizes that his son will not submit to his plan, so he turns him over to chastisement and lets his lust run its course. While the young man is "running his course," the Holy Spirit chastens him to repentance, restitution, and restoration. He wants to bring him over to the submission side of righteousness.

Luke 15:14-17   "But when he had spent all, there arose a severe famine in that land, and he began to be in want. Then he went and joined himself to a citizen of that country, and he sent him into his fields to feed swine. And he would gladly have filled his stomach with the pods that the swine ate, and no one gave him anything. But when he came to himself . . ."

The phrase "But when he came to himself . . ." means when he came to the end of his chastisement. This was the humbling part. It broke his strong will and the lust in his flesh. It was chastisement for the son to have to work for someone else.

If the son had died in his sinful living, he would still have gone to heaven. But God wants us to have something greater than just having eternal life. I am not belittling eternal life. God wants us to have a better life now, not waiting until we get to heaven.

Luke 15:17b-24 **". . .he said, 'How many of my father's hired servants have bread enough and to spare, and I perish with hunger! I will arise and go to my father, and will say to him, "Father, I have sinned against heaven and before you *[repentance]*, and I am no longer worthy to be called your son. Make me like one of your hired servants *[restitution]*."' And he arose and came to his father. But when he was still a great way off, his father saw him and had compassion, and ran and fell on his neck and kissed him *[restoration]*. And the son said to him, 'Father, I have sinned against heaven and in your sight, and am no longer worthy to be called you son.' But the father said to his servants, bring out the best robe and put it on him, and put a ring on his hand and sandals on his feet. And bring the fatted calf here and kill it, and let us eat and be merry; for this my son was dead and is alive again; he was lost and is found.' And they began to be merry. . . ."**
(Brackets mine.)

Look at what the chastisement did. The father released his son into the protection of the Holy Spirit for a life of chastisement, and it brought him to a place of submission.

Did you notice ". . .when he was still a great way off, his father saw him. . ."? This shows us that his father had been looking for him, waiting for him to come back. The father was so happy, he hugged and kissed his son, and said, "Let's have a party!"

Wait a minute, according to our "works" theology, shouldn't he be punished? No. Anybody who is living under submission has grace abounding. The son acknowledged that he couldn't live without his father's help.

That's all God is asking us to understand: we can't live in this life without His help.

Meanwhile, the second son is working in the fields night and day but only to be approved and earn blessing from the father.

Luke 15:25-29 **"Now his older son was in the field. And as he came and drew near to the house, he heard music and dancing. So he called one of the servants and asked what these things meant. And he said to him, 'Your brother has come, and because he has received him safe and sound, your father has killed the fatted calf.' But he was angry and would not go in. Therefore his father came out and pleaded with him. So he answered and said to his father, 'Lo, these many years I have been serving you; I never transgressed your commandment at any time; and yet you never gave me a young goat, that I might make merry with my friends.' "**

The second son was really saying, "Haven't I been working faithfully all these years to earn points with you? Don't I deserve at least the same treatment?"

Unfortunately, most Christians think this way. They believe right behavior wins things from God, and lack of right behavior loses things from God. That kind of theology is centered in works and not grace. It's not about the redemptive act of Christ. It's about what *you* can do!

Luke 15:30-32 **" 'But as soon as this son of yours came, who has devoured your livelihood with harlots, you killed the fatted calf for him.' And he said to him, 'Son, you are always with me, and all that I have is yours [you don't have to work for it, it's already yours]. It was right that we should make merry and be glad, for your brother was dead and is alive again, and was lost and is found.' "**
(Brackets mine.)

When the second son pointed out his relationship to the father, which was works (the law of performance), he still lacked because grace didn't abound in his life. He obeyed, but he lacked. He wasn't free. He was a slave to the lust of his mind.

The second son was jealous that his brother got to go out and play, while he had to stay home and work, ". . . not of works, lest anyone should boast."

Romans 6:15   "What then? Shall we sin because we are not under law but under grace? Certainly not!"

If I'm not under the law like the first son, should I go ahead and sin so that grace may abound? Certainly not! God doesn't want you to live out your sin, He wants you to submit your life.

CHAPTER 8

The Judgment of Sin

I personally believe that the most important thing you need to understand is that God loves you individually. When you relate to Him in a salvation relationship, you'll see the greatest spiritual growth in your life.

Our goal is not to live without sin. Our goal is to live by faith. Many Christians are living a life of trying to abstain from sin. Don't live a life of don'ts, live a life of *doing* faith. Anything that is not of faith is sin.

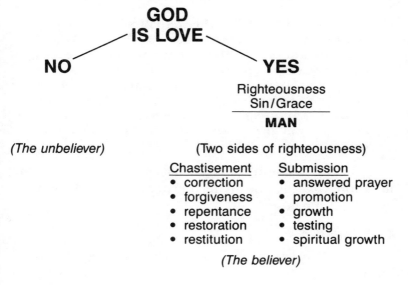

GOD IS LOVE

NO — **YES**

Righteousness
Sin / Grace

MAN

(The unbeliever)   (Two sides of righteousness)

Chastisement	Submission
• correction	• answered prayer
• forgiveness	• promotion
• repentance	• growth
• restoration	• testing
• restitution	• spiritual growth

(The believer)

Remember, under submission we have:
- answered prayer
- growth
- promotion
- testing
- spiritual growth

These people are living their lives by faith. They are majoring on the fruit of the Spirit. They want to concentrate on living by faith and being sensitive to the Holy Spirit.

Under the chastisement side we have:
- correction
- forgiveness
- repentance
- restitution
- restoration

God's purpose for chastisement is to bring a person to submission.

The law came to show man's weaknesses. When the law left, God sent the Holy Spirit. We do not live by the leading of the law, but by the leading of the Holy Spirit.

Romans 6:15-17   What then? Shall we sin because we are not under law but under grace? Certainly not! Do you not know that to whom you present yourselves slaves to obey, you are that one's slaves whom you obey, whether of sin leading to death, or of obedience leading to righteousness? But God be thanked that though you were slaves of sin, yet you obeyed from the heart that form of doctrine to which you were delivered.

Grace is not God's unmerited favor. Grace is God's love in action. Grace is God acting on your behalf to deliver you from an oppressor.

God, the Judge

The Bible calls God a judge. When hearing that word, most people think of the judge of today who sits behind a bench in a courtroom. Standing before God (the Judge), they picture themselves with Jesus on one side and the devil on the other side. People think that when a person is brought before God, the devil starts making accusations about him to God. God listens and frowns. Then He turns to Jesus and the person and says, "Is this true?" The person is about to say "yes," when suddenly, Jesus puts his hand over his mouth. Jesus says, "Father, he's one of Mine." Then the Father says, "Okay, since he's one of Yours, I'll pardon him."

If this is true, then we have not been redeemed. A pardon (or mistrial) is not redemption.

The problem with a pardon is that you leave the courtroom thinking you're guilty. A pardon can never remove the guilt complex, so you think you were released on a technicality. The result is you are now "living the abundant life" with pure guilt in your mind.

Let's think of a serial killer in court being tried for the murders he committed. A lawyer introduces some evidence that he obtained illegally, so the judge throws the case out of court. The serial killer goes free and they can't retry him. Now he's walking around on the streets, free. Everyone knows he's guilty. He knows he's guilty.

We have a lot of Christians walking around today with the same feeling of guilt. They know they are born again, but in their minds, there is no freedom from guilt. Why? Because they don't think they've lived up to the way God wants them to live.

Today's judges are supposed to be impartial, that is, someone who weighs the evidence on both sides and whoever is found wanting, is charged. Christians think that God does the same thing, weighs both sides, then finds the cross to be greater, and frees us. Please! Erase that whole scenario from your mind. That is not the judge of the Bible.

When you read the Old Testament, because it is "types and shadows" of the New Testament, you don't find a judge sitting there listening to both sides. Especially in the book of Judges, you'll find every judge with a delivering hand going against the enemy.

Psalm 75:7   But God is the Judge: He puts down one, And exalts another.

The one God puts down is the oppressor and the one He exalts is the oppressed.

Why would God want to listen to the devil? Through judgment, He puts down the oppressor, and lifts up the oppressed! The grace of God lifts us up.

Believers don't come to the judgment seat of God. We come to the reward seat of God. Unbelievers go to the judgment seat of God.

The grace of God judges the sin. God says, ''You've been oppressed by this. Let My delivering hand lift you up.'' God leads us out of the sin in our lives. He doesn't punish us for it. Christ was punished for it.

We are not going to pay the price that Jesus paid. Christ hung on the cross. My sin was put on Him. Why then would you think God would judge you for your sin? He will lead you out of it.

CHAPTER 9

Performance Lifestyle

Romans 7 is where many Christians live. Romans 7 tells about Christians who are outwardly conforming to the standard they think they should live in order to be accepted by God. They try to get closer to God by doing good works.

Because we all know the importance of prayer, we are taught to pray regularly. Some people have heard the teaching "pray one hour every day." That is okay to do, but have you ever missed one day of prayer and thought God was mad at you? Or maybe you thought He didn't love you as much?

Some Christians do not feel acceptance in the presence of God. They feel much too sinful to stand in His presence. Inside, they're living a life of guilt.

What people really want to know deep down inside is that God loves them.

I was reared in the Lutheran church, was born again in a Baptist church, and filled with the Spirit in an Assembly of God church. I had a religious upbringing that said I had to *do to get*. I just wanted God to say to me that He accepted me. I would pray a certain number of hours a day and read my Bible several hours a day. Inwardly, I never felt any better. I would do all of that but still go to bed at night and think, "I didn't go witness to anybody today, so I guess I won't be blessed."

I thought if I "did good," I'd be blessed, if I didn't, I'd be punished. It seemed like the more good I did, the more problems I found in me, and the worse I felt.

I was performing outwardly right behavior to gain acceptance. I was living a list of do's and don'ts to get God to bless me—or even just like me. When you live by a list, it will never end. Why? Because of the law.

We must start to think, "I am close to God already. Because I am close to God, I pray. Because I am close to God, I tithe. Because I am close to God, I read my Bible."

Living Under the Law

Romans 7:1-3 Or do you not know, brethren (for I speak to those who know the law), that the law has dominion over a man as long as he lives? For the woman who has a husband is bound by the law to her husband as long as he lives. But if the husband dies, she is released from the law of her husband. So then if, while her husband lives, she marries another man, she will be called an adulteress; but if her husband dies, she is free from that law, so that she is no adulteress, though she has married another man.

Paul is not teaching in Romans 7 about divorce. He does not change course during several chapters of very important teaching on salvation, Christians under the law, grace, etc., to begin a new subject.

Freed from the Law

Romans 7:4 Therefore, my brethren [you and I], you also have become dead to the law through the body of Christ, that you may be married to another—to Him who was raised from the dead, that we should bear fruit to God. (Brackets mine.)

We learned from these verses that the law has dominion over a man as long as he is alive. This means that if the man wants to please God, he must obey the law. We also know that no man can obey the law. The book of James tells us that if we transgress even one commandment, we have transgressed the whole law.

We now find ourselves in a dilemma. The dilemma is "I really want to do right for God, but the more I try to do right, the more I find myself falling short of what God wants."

You see, living under the law is actually living under a "performance lifestyle" where the Christian has a list made up in his mind (if I do this, this, this, and this). You may think that if you do those things, you will be pleasing to God so He will like you more and bless you more. The problem with that mindset is that every time you just about get your list completed, new items are added.

In Romans, Paul gives an example of a woman and a man. The woman has a husband who dies. She's then free to marry someone else. Paul tells us that we have died to the law. The law has not died, but we died because of our new birth in Jesus Christ. In fact, we not only died, we were born again in Jesus. Because of that, we are now free to "marry another."

The "another" whom we marry, in this example of Paul's, is the Spirit of life in Christ Jesus. This means our conformity is no longer based on the law, but on grace. I am now going to live in grace because of righteousness.

In verses 13 to 22, Paul declares that a Christian who really wants to do good for God, but believes he must live a performance lifestyle in order to attain that good level, will find himself frustrated.

> **Romans 7:14-15 For we know that the law is spiritual, but I am carnal, sold under sin. For what I am doing, I do not understand. For what I will to do, that I do not practice; but what I hate, that I do.**

Paul says here that I want to please God, so I try to practice pleasing God, but what I really practice is a performance lifestyle.

The performance lifestyle always causes me to come up short of the glory of God, therefore I feel condemned about my performance.

Romans 7:16   If, then, I do what I will not to do, I agree with the law that it is good.

Paul explains further that if my performance lifestyle leads me to the place of not achieving what I really want (being pleasing to God), then I have agreed that the law is good. It does exactly what it was created to do. The law was created to expose to man his inability to perform for God for the purpose of God's glory, blessings, or approval. But we are already approved in the eyes of God through grace.

Romans 7:17-18   But now, it is no longer I who do it, but sin that dwells in me. For I know that in me (that is, in my flesh) nothing good dwells; for to will is present with me, but how to perform what is good I do not find.

Paul declares that he really wants to do right for God and live in a relationship with Him, but in his flesh he doesn't have the ability to perform it.

Therefore Paul ends this chapter with "Who will help me?" He says in verse 25, "I thank God—through Jesus Christ our Lord!" He declares that it is Jesus Christ Who has delivered us from a performance lifestyle.

God is not looking for you to live a certain moral code—a performance lifestyle—for His approval. You have already been approved because of the resurrection of Jesus Christ. You already received His approval when you were born again because of your belief in Him.

Our lives will change because we are approved by God. We do not change our lives to get approved by God. The performance lifestyle is putting the cart before the horse. Christians who try to live that way will always be frustrated and disappointed.

CHAPTER 10

The Spiritual Believer

In Romans 6, 7, and 8, we have descriptions of Christians' spiritual states. Romans 6 describes the Christian controlled by sin. Romans 7 describes the Christian controlled by the law. Romans 8 describes the Christian living his life led by the Spirit.

God is love. There are two sides to the love of God. On the "no" side we have dead people being controlled by death. Death gives strength to sin. They're in a jail cell of sin. They have not said "yes" to Jesus Christ.

> **Romans 7:22-24   For I delight in the law of God according to the inward man. But I see another law in my members [law of sin and death], warring against the law of my mind [law of Spirit of life in Christ Jesus], and bringing me into captivity to the law of sin which is in my members. O wretched man that I am! Who will deliver me from this body of death?** (Brackets mine.)

There's a law connected to your flesh which is the *law of sin and death* (in "your members"). It causes your physical death, because when you were born again your physical body did not change.

There is another law which is connected to your spirit: the *law of the Spirit of life in Christ Jesus.*

The law of the Spirit of life in Christ Jesus has made us free from the law of sin and death. Before you were born again, you had no relationship with God. Sin and death controlled your life. When you became born again, you became alive to Christ and you now have a new law: the law of the Spirit of life in Christ Jesus.

You may ask, "Who is going to deliver me from this body of death?" Jesus Christ. If I want to serve the law of God, the law of the Spirit of life in Christ Jesus, I must make up my mind to order my behavior by the Spirit of God. In Christian terminology it's known as "walking in the Spirit." But if I close my mind, I will now serve the law of sin and death.

It is my choice. Do I want to develop in the law of the Spirit of life in Christ Jesus, or do I want to develop in the law of sin and death?

Romans 8:1   There is therefore now no condemnation to those who are in Christ Jesus . . .

The word "condemnation" means "a condemning sentence." There is no condemning sentence that will be carried out in Christ Jesus. This means I am free from the wrath of God.

Romans 8:2   For the law of the Spirit of life in Christ Jesus has made me free from the law of sin and death.

In order to activate or have the benefits of it, I need to continue in it. How did I begin my relationship with Jesus? I was born again. How did I become born again? By grace, not by works.

If I entered into the law of life by grace, then what allows me to continue in that law? Grace. The Holy Spirit leads me into this life of grace. I must be led by the Holy Spirit. God wants me to walk in the Spirit so I will not fulfill the lust of the flesh (Galatians 5).

Walking in the Spirit

These terms "walking in the flesh" and "walking in the Spirit" have confused a lot of Christians. They feel that the walk of the flesh is one of giving yourself over to horrible sin: murder, stealing, adultery, and more. On the other hand, they think that walking in the Spirit means you walk a perfect walk. No, you don't do either of those things.

If the law of sin and death is on the "no" side of God, and the law of the Spirit of life in Christ Jesus is on the "yes" side of God, what do you think the law of the Spirit of life is? In one word, it is "salvation."

How are you saved? You are saved by grace through faith. Salvation has two sides to it. My side is faith, God's side is grace. Grace is not God's unmerited favor.

Grace is defined as *God's love in action. God works on your behalf to right what is wrong.* Salvation is faith and grace working together. That is the law of the Spirit of life in Christ Jesus.

Here's what happens. Faith in God gives you His grace causing the law of sin and death to be removed.

The walk of the flesh is a walk of works. The walk of the Spirit is a walk of faith. It's really simple!

In the walk of the flesh, you're trying to do a list of works to get saved, or approved, and it's not going to happen. But, the faith side—walking in the Spirit—is walking in faith because you believe.

Don't think "If I do more things I'll be more spiritual and achieve more blessing from God. I'll pay my tithes and then I will be blessed." That's the walk of the flesh: works.

The person walking in the Spirit thinks "I am blessed. I believe it, so therefore I will respond to it as if it's already true. I am anointed because God has made me a king and priest. I will pay my tithes because I am blessed."

Do you see the difference?

The law gives man the instructions that are necessary to live for God. The reason the law cannot fulfill righteousness is because of the weakness of the man's flesh. So now we have a problem: flesh.

So God sent Jesus to condemn sin in the flesh. When Jesus died on the cross, God crucified the flesh and completely removed it from the relationship requirement. Flesh is not an issue in being related to God.

If there is no flesh, there is no requirement for the law to be fulfilled. Therefore God dealt with the flesh problem by crucifying Jesus on the cross. Romans 7 says we are "dead to the law."

Now when man becomes born again, his flesh dies, but his spirit becomes alive to God. Now he has the righteousness that the law had required in his flesh.

What do we do with this flesh issue? We still have our mortal bodies, but now the Spirit leads the flesh into the right relationship. We walk in the Spirit.

Walking in the Spirit is not a life of performance, it's a life of obedience and faith. It's responding to the voice of the Holy Spirit. We don't earn anything from God, because He's given all things to us.

Our relationship is always going to be by faith, so it can always be by grace. In faith, we are always going to believe that God has already accomplished everything for us.

Romans 8:4-8 . . . **that the righteous requirement of the law might be fulfilled in us who do not walk according to the flesh but according to the Spirit. For those who live according to the flesh set their minds**

**on the things of the flesh, but those who live accord-
ing to the Spirit, the things of the Spirit. For to be
carnally minded is death, but to be spiritually
minded is life and peace. Because the carnal mind
is enmity against God; for it is not subject to the law
of God, nor indeed can be. So then, those who are
in the flesh cannot please God.**

". . . those who are in the flesh cannot please God." How
do you please God? The Bible says you cannot please God
except by faith. That means that Romans 8:8 is a reciprocal
of Hebrews 11:6 which tells us we can only please God by
faith.

**Hebrews 11:6   But without faith it is impossible to
please Him, for he who comes to God must believe
that He is, and that He is a rewarder of those who
diligently seek Him.**

If we can't please God in the flesh, then we must be able
to please God in the spirit. The spirit and faith must be the
same thing.

It's not a mystical thing being "in the Spirit." Some people think it's some ultra, goose-bump, not-in-reality thing.
No, living in the Spirit is simply living by faith. Living by faith
means to believe and start living it. (We are going to respond
because it's already accomplished.)

A carnal mind will lead to death and destruction. But
to be spiritually minded is to walk in faith.

**Romans 8:10-11   And if Christ is in you, the body is
dead because of sin, but the Spirit is alive because
of righteousness. But if the Spirit of Him who raised
Jesus from the dead dwells in you, He who raised
Christ from the dead will also give life to your
mortal bodies through His Spirit who dwells in you.**

While you're living on the earth, God wants to work
in your mortal body and change you a little at a time. A little
more life, then a little more life.

Romans 8:12-15 Therefore, brethren, we are debtors—not to the flesh, to live according to the flesh. For if you live according to the flesh you will die; but if by the Spirit you put to death the deeds of the body, you will live. For as many as are led by the Spirit of God, these are sons of God. For you did not receive the spirit of bondage again to fear, but you received the Spirit of adoption by whom we cry out, "Abba, Father."

While you are being controlled by sin and death, it is the spirit of bondage that you fear. What are you fearing? You're fearing wrath (when you're not born again), but as a child of God, you haven't received this fear. You are walking in power, love, and a sound mind.

Romans 8:18-26 talk about how your body is suffering and how you go through different kinds of sufferings in this life. It talks about how different kinds of trials and pressure situations are designed to help change you and build character in your life. These things will help you develop. When you're in the midst of these things, you've been given the Holy Spirit to help you.

Romans 8:26a   Likewise the Spirit also helps in our weaknesses.

The Spirit and our bodies walk together in faith. We will walk with Him because we are delivered children of God. The Holy Spirit will quicken our mortal bodies. He will take the salvation that is inside our spirits, work it into our flesh, and then work it through our life's situations.

When I see weaknesses in my flesh (while I'm walking in faith) and situations that seem to be overtaking me, the Holy Spirit helps me! He helps me with groanings that cannot be uttered. The Holy Spirit knows my every weakness and intercedes by calling on the heart of God. He searches my heart and finds out why I am weak. He begins to communicate to me about my weak areas, showing me how to turn them into victories.

He's not coming to *condemn* me because I'm weak. He's coming to *deliver* me because I'm weak!

So many ministers are standing in pulpits today pointing their fingers at people saying, "You filthy Christian, how dare you have sin in your life." We have sin in our lives because we still have a mortal body! God isn't finished with our complete deliverance. He's given His Spirit, not to condemn us, but to help us.

God gave us the Holy Spirit to help us overcome our covetousness, help us overcome our greed, help us overcome our jealousy, help us overcome our habitual behavior, help us overcome our addiction to any substance or addictive thing, and help us overcome our codependency on people.

When we yield to the Holy Spirit, He speaks to us and helps us. When we find we can't be nice to someone, He says, "You can be nice to that person." The Holy Spirit is there to help us walk through it. He helps pick us up when we fall.

He will make everything work out for our good because we're going to walk in faith and not works. If we're walking in faith but fall down, we get back up in faith. Even if we mess it up, God is going to turn it around and make it work out for our good.

In Romans 8:38 & 39, Paul says there's nothing that can separate us from the love of God. If none of those things can separate us, how can sin? God isn't going to stop loving you because of sin.

As you humble yourself under the mighty hand of God, He will exalt you in due time. As you learn the things that are necessary to overcome the flesh and continue to walk in faith, you will see victory.

Paul the Apostle wanted to quit at one time. "I don't know if I should stay or go." (Philippians 1:21-24) He had to go into prayer about it. After all of the beatings, shipwrecks and other things that happened to him, he finally said, "God, would You remove this thorn in my flesh?'' God said, ''My grace is sufficient for you. My love in action is enough.''

And so it is for us when we find ourselves overwhelmed, overtaken, or burned out. We now know that His grace is sufficient. God's grace is His love in action to help you. God is working in your life to change what is wrong and make it right because He loves you—yes, YOU!—so very much.

ABOUT POWER LIVING MINISTRIES

Power Living Ministries helps people change their lives. They have the vision of getting the message of God's love to as many people as possible through the publishing of books and tapes. To accomplish this vision, Power Living Ministries is prayerfully and financially supported by people like you.

If you feel a call by God to be a part of this vision, we invite you to receive more information by writing or calling:

Power Living Ministries
1026 S. East Street
Anaheim, CA 92805
(800) 435-2627

ABOUT THE AUTHOR

Tom Barkey pastors Power Community Church in Anaheim, California. He and his wife, Linda, began the church in 1979. The Barkeys and their six children live in Yorba Linda, California.

Tom is known for his emphasis on the Father's love and grace. His common-sense approach and humor are prominent in his teaching of God's Word.